What do <u>you</u> want to know?

Read this book to learn

how selling works,

why customers buy,

and how to sell anything.

You **can be better at selling!**

You made it this far. Now please take the next step and buy this book. This is an easy-to-understand book that will teach you the basic concepts of selling. With basics, you can be a better salesperson. You can be more persuasive in everything you do!

www.alphabeticalbasicconcepts.com

Alphabetical Basic Concepts of Selling

Dale Brakhage

Published by Lulu.com

www.lulu.com

All rights reserved.

Copyright © 2007 by Dale Brakhage

This book may not be reproduced in whole or in part, by electronic or any other means, without permission. For information www.alphabeticalbasicconcepts.com

Library of Congress Control Number: 2007907467

ISBN: 978-1-4303-2740-0

Cover Art by Alan Moore

Manufactured in the United States of America

Contents

	Page
Dedication	7
Introduction	8
How this Book Works for You.	11
A is for Ask	13
B is for Benefits	20
C is for Customers	23
D is for Dedication	28
E is for Enthusiasm	32
F is for First Impression	37
G is for Goal	42
H is for Honesty	45
I is for Inventory	48
J is for Join	52
K is for Knowledge	56
L is for Listening	60
M is for More	67
N is for No	70
O is for Organization	76
P is for Price	80
Q is for Questions	84
R is for Relationships	90

Contents continued

	Page
S is for Service	95
T is for Territory	98
U is for Up Selling	102
V is for Value	105
W is for Want	109
X is for X-factor	112
Y is for Yes	118
Z is for Zebra	123
In Closing	126
About the Author	127

Dedication

This book is dedicated to all the kids who ever tried to sell candy bars, cookies, cleaning stuff, magazines, light bulbs and anything else for their school, band, scout troop or club.

It is especially dedicated to the parents, neighbors and friends who bought that stuff, not because they needed it, but because they wanted to help those kids!

Introduction

Do you want to know why selling is important?

Here is your answer. Take a deep breath. Now, let it out. Air is rapidly becoming the only thing not sold. You buy (and somebody sells) your food, clothing, furniture, home, office, car, telephone, air conditioning, heat, electric lights and even the water you drink.

Look around you for a moment. Can you see any object near you that has never been sold? That is why selling is so important. Selling touches everything around us, and we are all involved in buying and selling things. Selling also includes persuading others to accept your ideas. In *every* type of sale, certain events happen. An item or an idea is offered, and when the seller and buyer agree on its value, the buyer pays and accepts ownership. It does not matter what is for sale, from soup spoons to super computers, the basic concepts of selling apply.

If you understand the basic concepts of how any sale works, the mystery of selling disappears. If you take away the mystery, the stress of selling goes away. The purpose of this book is to de-mystify selling. This book explains in simple language what selling is and how selling works.

Introduction

When you understand how selling works, including what makes a customer buy, you sell more. As you sell more, selling becomes fun. Applying the basics of selling makes you an effective salesperson. You sell more, you earn more money and you win recognition for your success. Get the basics right, and all the rest falls into place.

This book explains the basic concepts of selling. It assigns one basic concept to each of the 26 letters of the alphabet. That makes them easier to remember. Do not worry. You do not have to memorize anything. You certainly do not have to use all 26 basics every time you want to sell something! Just as you choose the right few letters of the alphabet to spell different words, you choose the right few sales basics to make different sales. Every selling situation is unique. Use only the sales basics you need to make that sale.

As you learn the basic concepts of selling, you will see that they apply to any selling situation. Selling is simply trying to persuade others to believe in the value of your ideas. Use these basic concepts, and you will become much more persuasive in everything you do. Note: after you have learned to use all 26 basic concepts of selling, it is a good idea to read other sales books to add more techniques to your strong foundation of selling basics.

Imagine trying to read and write using only five or six letters. You might get your point across, but using more letters makes writing easier. It is the same for selling. Many salespeople use only five or six of these basic concepts of selling. They miss so much business! Use ten of these basic concepts to be more effective than using only five. Use all 26 to excel in sales.

The alphabet contains only 26 letters. Those letters, used in various combinations, can write any word known to man. The entire Bible uses only those 26 letters! Shakespeare wrote his great works with the exact same 26 letters that you use every day, the same letters that first graders use! The only difference between "To be, or not to be," and "See Spot run," is the skill of the writer.

Skill develops through practice and study. Everyone sells. You can sell more effectively *if* you learn the basic concepts of selling *and* practice using them. To receive the most benefit from these concepts, read them several times. When you understand them, try using them in different combinations to see what works best for you. Work to fit one more of them into your selling every day. Then, watch your sales and your income grow as you become a skilled seller!

How this book works for you.

The structure of this book is not as important as how you want to learn the information.

This book design makes your learning easy. The basic concepts of selling appear in alphabetical order, a simple structure. We all know it, and it makes the concepts easier to remember.

Some of the basic concepts relate to others that do not appear next in the alphabetical order. You may want to learn more about those related concepts right away. Since what you want to learn (and when you want to learn it) is more important than the structure of this book, you have the option of turning directly to the related concept. To help you do that, the first time any related concept appears in this book, it appears in CAPITAL LETTERS. For example, ASK is the first basic concept. When the related concept, QUESTIONS first appears, it is in capital letters. If you want, you can turn immediately to the questions chapter and learn more about it. You may prefer to skip around, learning about the related concepts instead of reading this book in order. That is perfectly all right! The important thing is for you to learn, and then put these basic concepts of selling to work for you.

Here is another way other way this book works for you. It gives you breaks! Occasionally, you will find an interesting tidbit of information that will take your mind off the basic concepts. It is not enough to distract you from your learning. It is just enough to give your brain a break. Think of these breaks like the ones you enjoyed when you were in school.

Your key to success with this book is to read *all* the basic concepts. Then you will understand how they all fit together. Understand the big picture, and then begin using a few of the concepts. Try the concepts that make the most sense to you first. After you get comfortable using those, add a few more. Read about them again, and then use them in your selling. The more basic concepts you use, the more persuasive you will be. You will sell more and earn more money, too.

Welcome to this book, the <u>Alphabetical Basic Concepts of Selling</u>. On the next page, you begin learning the basic concepts of how to sell anything. Good luck as you put these concepts to work for you!

A is for Ask

Ask and they will buy.

Versus

Don't ask don't sell.

Asking is the first basic of every sale. Asking can be as simple as the gasoline pump flashing "Carwash? Yes or No" on a tiny video screen before it prints your receipt. On the other hand, asking can be as complicated as a contract hundreds of pages long used to sell the Navy a new aircraft carrier.

Asking connects you with another person. Everyday, people pass right by you without making direct contact. When you ask someone a QUESTION, however, you make a connection. You capture that person's attention. When you, as a seller, ask a buyer to give you something in exchange for whatever you are selling, you establish a link. Then it is up to that other person to answer your question. They can say YES or NO, or they can say maybe. They can even ignore you, but for a moment, you have their attention. They connect with you, and they are thinking about you because you asked them a question. It is that simple. When you ask someone a question, you connect. It does not matter if what you are selling is expensive or cheap. Your question can be ordinary, such as "You want fries with that?" It can be life changing, such as "Will you marry me?" Whatever you are asking, when you ask, they respond. Asking the question starts it all.

Asking is fundamental to selling. Do you agree that, if all else is equal, salespeople who ask 10 CUSTOMERS to buy something will sell MORE than salespeople who ask only five customers? Yes, they will, every time, because selling is a numbers game. Ask more sell more. Not only is it important to ask many people, it is important to ask every customer you see to buy your product. It is easy to become involved in a nice conversation with a customer and get distracted away from selling. Remember why you are there, to sell something, and remember to ask every customer to buy today. You sell more by asking more.

How you ask is important. Be polite. Be direct, and before you ask, make certain you give your customer a good reason to say yes. On the next page are three examples of how to ask a customer to buy something. The basic selling situation in this example is how most of us made our first sale, so it is an appropriate starting point

Three elementary school students are selling candy bars door-to-door to raise money for their school. The first student just asks, "Do you WANT to buy a candy bar?" The second student says, "Hi. I am selling candy bars for my school. Would you please buy one from me today?" The third student says, "Mrs. Jones, my teacher at school really needs a new computer, and if we all sell 30 candy bars, we can buy her one right away. They are one dollar each. Would you like to buy two or three?"

The first student will sell some candy bars if he asks enough neighbors. Most people do not sit at home waiting to buy candy bars, but enough people like candy, so he will sell some. The second student will sell more than the first, because people who like candy will see a chance to help her school. She gave them a reason to buy. The third student will sell even more. He pleasantly and briefly explained why he is selling and what he is selling. He gives customers a chance to help him, his teacher and his school. They even get candy out of the deal! Did you notice that he asked them to buy two or three? He understands selling!

Before a customer will buy your product or SERVICE, they must understand what they are buying and what the PRICE will be. You present those details in a conversation before you ask them to buy.

It makes sense, does it not, to tell customers what the product and price are before you ask them to buy? Asking them to buy usually comes at the end. In a sales presentation, asking the customer to buy is "the close." You close your selling presentation by asking them to buy. Look at these examples of questions that ask customers to buy. They are quite different, but they all get to the same point, please buy.

> Would you like to buy this now?
>
> Would you prefer a red one or a blue one?
>
> Can I wrap this up for you?
>
> Will that be cash or credit card?

Some closing questions work better than others, but all of them work better than not asking. If you put two salespeople on the street selling cookies, and one of them just stands there saying nothing and the other asks everyone, "You wouldn't want to buy some of these today, would you?", the asker will sell more cookies, guaranteed.

Some people feel uncomfortable directly asking other people to buy something. This is common and is more a fear of the unknown than a fear of selling. The unknown is what the customer is going to say. They may say yes, or they may say no. Professional salespeople realize that more people are going to say no than yes. (Realistically, if all customers said yes all the time, there would be no need for salespeople! Every business would sell everything it could make. That never happens, so salespeople will always have jobs.)

The best salespeople know that the more people they ask, the more times they will hear yes. They will also hear no, but that is okay. Salespeople understand that many people say no. When you are selling, every "No thanks," brings you closer to hearing a "Yes, I'll buy that." Train yourself to *expect* yes on every call. At the same time, train yourself to not allow the word no to disappoint you.

You can learn something from every customer, the ones that buy and the ones who do not buy. After each sales call you make, take a moment to think about what happened. How did the customer react to what you said? As you evaluate your selling, you will discover that some words sell better than others do. Use them again. Experiment with the way you present your products and ask for the sale. As more customers say yes, keep revising your questions to make them more effective.

Note: there is a big difference between selling and order taking. For example, when you bring your groceries to the checkout line in a grocery store, the grocery clerk does not ask you if you want to purchase. She understands that you want to pay the marked price for those goods. Order taking is simply taking money from customers that have already decided to buy. Salespeople can certainly take an order, but that is not really selling. Selling is persuading others to buy from you. The other 25 basic concepts of selling that can make you more persuasive appear in the rest of this book.

Take a break! **Selling Happens Everywhere!**

Professional salespeople earn their living by selling their company's products. Politicians win elections by "selling" the public on voting for them. Religious leaders grow their groups by "selling" people on believing in a particular way. Single people get dates by "selling" other people on the idea of going out with them. When two people like each other enough, they "sell" each other on the idea of getting married. Parents "sell" their idea of how to live a happy and productive life to their children. Families visit a particular movie or restaurant after someone in the family "sells" the others on the idea.

As you can see, selling goes on all the time. In fact, you have been selling all your life, even if you did not realize it. Everyone sells!

Anytime you try to persuade another person that you have a valuable idea, you are selling. That is much different from the picture in most people's minds when you mention selling - a very slick, pushy, fast talking man in a plaid sports coat trying to sell beat up cars to anybody who happens to walk by his used car lot!

A very small percentage of people sell products professionally. Welcome, sisters and brothers in selling! For you, this book is a quick and easy review of the basic behaviors that make selling work. Professional salespeople know a regular review of the basics helps you keep your selling skills sharp. Since you have not seen the basics in this form before, the review should be interesting. Please let me know what you thought of this book when you are done reading it.

Most people, however, "sell" every day as amateurs. They are the ones simply persuading voters, congregations, friends, fiancée's, children, etc. to believe in the VALUE of an idea. This book will open their eyes to how selling works and show them how to be more persuasive. Those people (most people) can see the biggest positive changes in their lives from applying these basic concepts. Please recommend this book to as many of those amateurs as you can. They will thank you for it. I would like to hear from you as well when you are done reading this book. That is the end of your first break. Everyone go back to class!

B is for Benefits

Facts tell; benefits sell.

Facts are words you use to tell other people *what* your product is. Benefits are words you use to tell other people what your product does for them. Benefits are much stronger selling words than facts. Why is that? Because we buy something after we believe it will do good things for us, not before. The moment we start to believe that something, anything, will provide a benefit for us (do something good for us), we begin to WANT it. When we want something enough, we buy it.

Do you see that people buy things for what the product can do? We buy light bulbs for the benefit of seeing after dark. We buy trashcans for the benefit of not having stinky trash all over our house. We buy coffee for the benefit of waking up and feeling alert. We buy insurance for the benefit of feeling secure about the future.

We buy gasoline, not because it is poisonous, smells terrible and can easily explode, but because it fuels our cars so we can travel wherever we want to go. The facts about gasoline do not make anyone want to buy it. However, the benefit gasoline provides, traveling, makes us buy it. We keep buying it, even though the price keeps going higher and higher. People will keep buying gasoline until there is some other convenient way for them to travel.

Here is a comparison of facts and benefits. Consider a cell phone.

Facts	Benefits
It is small.	You can carry it with you easily and stay in touch.
It is plastic.	It is tough. Drop it, and it will not break like glass.
It has numbers.	You can talk to the world by pushing the numbers.
It has a battery.	You are free to use it anywhere you want to go.
It stores data.	Important phone numbers are always there for you.

Do you see the difference between facts and benefits? Facts just tell about something. Facts are all about your product. Benefits are all about your customer. Benefits show how your customer's life will be better! When you are the customer buying a product, are you interested in it, or what it will do for you?

To discover the benefits of your product or service, state a fact about it and then ask, "So what does this do to help the customer?" An even easier way is to ask, "So what?" In the cell phone example above, the first fact was, "It is small." So what? You can carry it with you easily and stay in touch with your friends, family, co-workers, etc. As you can see, a benefit is the, "So what?" for a fact. A benefit explains to customers what the product does for them.

To sell anything quickly, always describe the benefits to your customer. Put yourself in your buyer's place for a moment, JOIN their world and imagine what challenges that customer must face. Ask them what they want the product to do for them. They will tell you. As you describe the benefits, you describe how your product helps the customer solve problems and be happier. When you are talking about benefits, you are talking about your customers instead of about your product. It is all about them. Customers will appreciate your help.

To be more persuasive, always follow a fact with a benefit. Explain what good things the product will do. If your customer agrees, they will want to buy your product. A thousand facts will not make a customer want to buy your product. One good benefit will.

C is for Customers

Selling would be so easy if we could

do it without all those customers!

Successful selling is all about customers. The product you are selling is not the most important thing in your sale. The most important thing is what your customers want your product to do for them. When they believe your product has a benefit for them, they will buy it.

Where do you find customers? They come from everywhere. To find your customers, just put yourself in their place. For example, if you are selling jewelry, think to yourself, "Where would I be if I wanted to buy jewelry?" The answer is obvious, in a jewelry store. To sell jewelry, you set up a jewelry store. If you are selling hot dogs, you can find hungry customers at baseball parks, city corners at lunchtime, etc. If you are selling the latest incredible kitchen gadget, you can find millions of customers watching their TVs late at night, so run a TV infomercial.

Your next question is, "How would I want to be treated if I were a customer?" The answer to that question is a little tougher. Not everyone wants to be treated the same. Fortunately, almost all customers want to receive friendly service. They want to be recognized, and they want to receive respect. They absolutely want fairness and HONESTY, and they all want to get the best value for their money.

All sales begin at the beginning, the FIRST IMPRESSION. Salespeople have three seconds to make a positive first impression. Three seconds is all it takes for a customer to decide whether or not they like you. To create a good first impression, have a neat appearance and smile! Greet the customers with ENTHUSIASM and warmth. The customer will glance at you and make an immediate judgment based on your appearance and your attitude (your sincere desire to be of service). This immediate judgment by customers is the best reason salespeople should always dress for success. That means always wear your nicest clothes and your best attitude to work.

The best salespeople *immediately* greet customers in a friendly manner, and at the same time, evaluate every customer's response to the greeting. You can see right away whether or not a customer wants personal attention. Pay attention to the customer's body language. If this new customer moves toward you and begins a conversation with you, it is safe to stay closer. If the customer moves away from you with a gesture or an unresponsive reply, it is better for you to give them their space. Be ready to assist that customer when they indicate they want your help.

No two customers act alike. One can never predict how a customer will act by their appearance. Importantly, one can never pre-judge a customer's ability to purchase by their appearance. Today, millionaires can dress like homeless people, and homeless people can dress like millionaires. Treat all new customers the same and never underestimate their ability to buy until you have done a credit check!

Without customers, there are no sales. Everything salespeople say or do should focus on what the customer wants. Incredibly though, many salespeople focus on themselves. They are more concerned with selling their product than they are with what the customer wants. Customers do not respect these "pushy" salespeople. Self-centered salespeople sell less than "customer oriented" salespeople do. Customers want you to care more about them, less about yourself.

This is important! Before you say anything or show any product, think to yourself, "What does this customer want?" Obviously, if you do not know what that customer wants, you need to ask. In the chapter on questions, you will find tips on exactly how to ask a customer what they want. Once you know what the customers want to buy, you can show the products with benefits that will satisfy them.

It takes much more work to gain a new customer than it does to keep an old customer. Old customers, regular customers, repeat customers, are the foundation of any business. On the average, 80% of any business comes from 20% of the customers. That is the 80/20 rule of sales, and it highlights how important repeat customers are for you.

Repeat customers should be treated with more respect and attention than new customers should. Be careful! Sometimes it is the easy to take your repeat customers for granted. Do not let that happen. Remember, other salespeople are doing their best to turn your repeat customers into their new customers!

Here is one last thing about customers. Everyone agrees that people who trade their money for your product are customers. Life, however, is about so much more than that! *Everyone* is a customer. Everyone has something to give you, and you should treat everyone like customer.

Your parents and your children have respect they can give you, or not; treat them like customers. Your spouse has love he/she can give you, or not; treat your spouse like a customer. Your co-workers have help and support they can provide you, or not; treat them like customers. Your mail carrier, your barber, your garbage man, etc. can all provide you with excellent service, or not; treat them as you would a customer to get great service. Even your pets can give you love and attention, or not. Please be certain to treat your pets like customers!

How much better would this world be if all its leaders treated their people and other countries like customers?

D is for Dedication

The suitcase of success!

At any busy airport, you will see business people hurrying to their destinations pulling a small black suitcase on wheels. Those little suitcases all have tiny wheels and pull out handles. They are small, but they have extra pockets and zippers so a person can carry everything he/she needs on their trip. Experienced businesspeople learn how to pack those suitcases with exactly the things they need. There is no room for anything extra. Dedication is like those little black suitcases on wheels.

Dedication helps you focus on the things you need on your trip to success. Dedication teaches you to leave behind the extra things you do not really need. Once you learn how to use it, dedication makes your journey to success much easier. So, how does dedication work and how do you learn to use it?

Dedication is focusing your thoughts and actions to accomplish something. Actions are a tremendously important part of dedication.

Simply focusing your thoughts without taking action is only meditation. Taking action accomplishes things. Thinking about it never sold anything. You must take action to make things happen.

People who win awards for great accomplishments always receive great praise for their dedication. It does not matter how long it took to accomplish the deed. For example, a retiree receiving a gold watch for 20 years of service and a soldier receiving a medal for one hour of extreme bravery in battle both receive praise for their dedication. The common thread in both examples is <u>action</u>. Those people took action that accomplished great things.

How does dedication work? First, you decide you are going to be successful. That is a choice you must consciously make, like deciding to go on a trip. Second, you must decide what actions you must take to be successful. Third, you focus on those actions, and you get them done. If you succeed the first time, that is great! If you do not succeed, you try again. You keep trying until you accomplish what you decided to do. That is persistence. Persistence overcomes all obstacles. The best example of persistence is the Grand Canyon. For centuries, water persistently flowing through the canyon washed away the rock and dug what is now one of the wonders of the natural world.

Persistence is a result of dedication. Persistence is one of the most powerful tools of life. It comes with a 100% guarantee. If you persist in taking the actions required to accomplish your GOAL, if you do not quit, then you have a 100% better chance of accomplishing your goal then anybody who quits. Persistence pays!

When you focus on just the actions you must take to succeed, and when you avoid activities that will not help you reach your goal, then you are dedicated. You spend your valuable time doing the things that will get you closer to your desired result. Dedication helps you succeed faster than other people who get distracted by other activities. Dedication helps you focus on the things you need to succeed, and it helps you leave unimportant things behind you. Just like one of those little black airport suitcases, dedication helps you move swiftly and easily toward where you want to be in your life.

Take a break! **Why did Dale write this book?**

I love building things. When I was a kid, I built model cars. As a teenager, I discovered real cars! There is *nothing* better than taking something apart to figure out how it works, and then making it work better (alright, making it *go faster*. It is the same thing!)

D is for Dedication

When I earned a degree in Educational Psychology, I enjoyed studying how learning works and how people change their behavior to make their lives work better. As I began my career in sales, I applied that understanding of psychology to sales work. Immediately, I observed differences in the behavior of award winning salespeople and other salespeople. It was easy to adopt that behavior and succeed in sales.

After over 30 years of success selling, managing and training, I wanted a new challenge. Our two children were off in college, so I had time to accomplish something new, like discovering the secret to selling *anything!* That would be a great accomplishment. I decided to go for it.

First, I used my training in educational psychology to analyze the complex process of selling to discover exactly how selling works. I took selling apart, and broke it down into its basic concepts. Working at night and on weekends, I did it. (I thought it might take a week or two, but it took years!) In any case, I got it done. I had the secret to selling anything, the basic concepts of selling! That was neat, but could I explain them in a simple way so anyone could learn to apply them and sell better? Absolutely, they are *basic* concepts. What I needed to do next was fit them into a system that everyone could identify with, like the alphabet! More nights and weekends later, here it is! I hope you like it. OK, everybody, this break is over. It is time to get back to learning more of the alphabetical basic concepts of selling!

E is for Enthusiasm!

Yes indeed, enthusiasm sells!

Enthusiasm is the energy of a positive attitude overflowing out of a person. You can see enthusiasm in how a person sits, stands, walks and talks. You can see enthusiasm in the expression on their face, and in how many hours they work each day. You can spot an enthusiastic person a mile away. Whenever people are obviously positive about something, we call them enthusiastic.

The most important thing about enthusiasm in selling is this - enthusiasm is contagious! You can catch enthusiasm two ways: from other people, and from your dreams. Enthusiastic people infect others with their positive energy. It flows from their smiling faces, their energetic talk and their obvious passion for their cause. If they have a great product, that is good. Even if they have a poor product, enthusiasm itself can make customers take notice.

Customers will respond well to your positive enthusiasm (as long as you do not overwhelm them with it!) Customers will overlook small flaws in your sales presentation if you are selling with enthusiasm. Your positive energy is the key to their acceptance. Most people are attracted to positive energy from another person. As you would expect, most people avoid others who are acting negatively. This is the most important reason why salespeople need to keep a positive attitude. Your positive attitude expresses itself as enthusiasm, and that enthusiasm attracts customers who will catch your enthusiasm for your product.

How do you develop enthusiasm? First, catch it from others. Hang out with enthusiastic people and avoid negative people. Read books written by enthusiastic authors. Watch enthusiastic people on TV, and open yourself up to their positive attitudes. Second, catch enthusiasm from your dreams. Think about your dream of success. Imagine yourself as successful. See your success in your mind and feel how good it will be. The positive power of your dreams and imagination will fuel your enthusiasm.

It takes a while to build enthusiasm. You should not expect to become truly enthusiastic overnight. It takes practice. You can act enthusiastically any time you choose. You can decide at any moment to think positively or negatively about any situation. When you choose to be positive, you will find it easier to be enthusiastic. The positive power spilling out of an enthusiastic person comes from their positive thoughts. Here is how it works. First, focus your mind on positive thoughts such as:

> This is a good product.
>
> This product will sell.
>
> Customers will buy from me today.
>
> I will be successful in this job.

Second, reject any negative thoughts such as:

> This will not work.
>
> No way I can sell this.
>
> Nobody is going to buy this.

Since you can only think one thought at a time, you can train your brain to think positively. When a negative thoughts starts, and they will (everybody gets negative thoughts), immediately tell yourself to forget that. Say it aloud to emphasize the point. (If you are not alone, be ready to explain that you are building enthusiasm. Otherwise, people might think you are a little crazy.) Then, deliberately replace that negative thought with an obviously positive one. It is just like writing, when you erase a mistake and rewrite it correctly. Here is an example. You are driving home from work, and the negative thought pops into your head that another car might crash into you. Immediately, recognize that as a negative thought. Then, deliberately think to yourself, "Forget that!" Then consciously replace that negative thought with the mental picture of you safely arriving at home.

If a negative thought like, "He is not going to buy this," pops into your head before you see a customer, erase it! Forget that thought and replace it with a thought of the customer saying yes.

After a while, maybe weeks or months, you will be so aware of positive and negative thinking that you will nearly always think positively. In time, thinking positively will become a great habit, and a forceful tool for better living. When your brain is full of positive thoughts, energy from those thoughts spills out in the form of enthusiastic actions. You smile, and you speak with friendliness and confidence. You feel better, too. Your body language confirms to your customers that you know what you are talking about here. Your customers notice your positive energy, and that is when it happens, they catch your enthusiasm!

Here is one word about trying to fake it. Stop. If you have truly negative thoughts about what you are selling, then stop. Customers will avoid your bad attitude and false enthusiasm. To get back on track with genuine enthusiasm, take some time to think positive thoughts about what you are selling. Get help from other enthusiastic people. Learn what they think to get positive and enthusiastic about the product. Find something to be enthusiastic about, and then you can genuinely become enthusiastic.

As you work to become more positive and enthusiastic, your sales results will improve. Your success will make you even more enthusiastic. How powerful is enthusiasm? Consider this. People who have all the physical, mental and spiritual tools to win can <u>fail</u> without enthusiasm. On the other hand, people with very few tools for success will succeed if they enthusiastically keep trying. Others will catch that enthusiasm and help them succeed.

By the way, do you remember that customers include your family, coworkers, friends and neighbors? They will also enjoy your enthusiasm. Positive, enthusiastic people are fun to be near. Of course, this means you will need to become positive and enthusiastic about all aspects of your life. Go head! You will be a happier healthier person for it.

F is for First Impression

Meet the 3-second sale.

You have three seconds or less to make a good first impression on customers. It does not matter if they are seeing you in person, listening to you on the phone or reading your letter or e-mail message. They decide to like you or not in the first three seconds.

If you make a good first impression, the customer is more likely to listen to what you have to say. So what makes a good first impression? A professional image works best. Two things are very important for your professional image: your overall appearance and your smile.

Your overall appearance includes your grooming, posture and clothing. You should always appear clean and well groomed. Stand up straight, and sit with good posture. When you appear healthy, happy and alert, you impress business professionals.

To select what to clothing to wear, let your surroundings tell you what will fit in the best. If you are calling on professionals in office buildings, a business suit will work. If you are calling on industrial workers in shops, slacks and a golf shirt will project the right image. If you are selling for a charity group and have a uniform, wear it proudly and correctly. Successful salespeople learn that they can fit in with their customers and project a professional image at the same time.

Customers make their first impression based upon how well you fit into their idea of what a good salesperson should look like, or sound like or write like. First impressions really are not about you. First impressions are really about how your customers <u>perceive</u> you.

If that is true, how can any salesperson guess what every single one of their customers wants to see and hear? You win by playing the odds. Salespeople know what most customers want to see. They want to see a smiling, clean, well-groomed and professional salesperson. They look for someone who genuinely cares more about what customers want to buy than what salespeople want to sell. All customers want a salesperson that will be able to help them solve their problems.

Customers make a new first impression of you every time they see you. Even if you have established a friendship with the customers, they still assess you every time they see you. They decide immediately if they are going to spend time listening to you that day, so it is very important for you to make that good first impression.

So how exactly do you make a good first impression? Inside sales people working in stores make a good first impression by letting customers identify them easily. Wear your uniform or name badge proudly. Pay attention to the customers. Smile at them and speak as soon as you see them. Let them know you are prepared to help them whenever they are ready for help. The absolute worst thing you can do as an inside sales person is ignore a customer. Customers are more likely to buy a product if they know you are ready and willing to help them when they need you. On the other hand, if customers feel like you cannot be bothered to help them, they will go somewhere else. They will find another store and a more attentive salesperson to take their money.

If you are an outside sales person, you travel to see your customers. The most important thing for you to remember about first impressions is this - be ready. You often have to wait to see the decision maker. Know when your customer will first be able to see you, or hear you. You do not want to appear distracted or daydreaming when the customer appears. That projects a first impression of "I'm not ready."

Customers want to do business with salespeople who are always ready to help them. So be on the lookout. If you are waiting outside a door, stay alert to hear the customer coming. If you are in a waiting room, be ready when they call you. If you are waiting in the customer's office, stay alert to hear the customer coming.

When your customer can see you, speak up with a smile and a friendly greeting. Say their name if you know how to pronounce it correctly. Everyone is attracted to the sound of his or her name. Congratulations! You just made a positive first impression, and you are on your way to making your sale.

Take a break!

Oh, no! Someone expects you to sell something!

If you are reading this book, you have probably felt this way. There is a natural sense of stress that comes with a sales goal, no matter if your goal is to sell a box of cookies or a million dollars of real estate. That stress comes from three unknowns:

>Who is going to buy it?

>How am I going to sell it?

>When will they buy?

That stress is normal. Everyone feels it. The good news is this; you can reduce stress by eliminating the unknowns.

Successful salespeople work with very little stress. They know and understand the basic concepts of selling, so they already know the answers to two of the three questions above. They were not born with that KNOWLEDGE. They learned it through training and years of experience. When professional salespeople go to work, they know who is likely to buy and how they are going to sell. They have eliminated two of the three unknowns. How can they do that? They apply basic sales concepts that apply to every sales situation. The only unknown left is "When will they buy?" With the stress significantly reduced, the sales job becomes fun. Successful salespeople love to go to work because they can enjoy their jobs with hardly any stress. The sales goal is always there, of course. The work, however, is always easier when you have the right tools, like the alphabetical basic concepts of selling.

Ok, back to learning. The break is over.

G is for Goal

How can you get there

if you do not know where you are going?

An old saying states that a journey of 1000 miles begins with the first step. That same journey, if the proper goal is set before you start, may take only 500 miles! A goal is, in its simplest form, deciding precisely where you want to go. People moving toward a goal get there faster than people who are just moving.

The first thing you do every morning is set a goal. When you first wake up, you set a goal for what you are going to do next. You may decide to hit "snooze" and get 10 minutes of sleep. You may decide to hop out of bed and head for the coffee pot. Either way, you decide, then you move. That is the simplest example of goal setting. You use the same process to make yourself successful at selling. You decide what to do, then you set a goal to do it. Goals work by focusing your actions.

G is for Goal

"I'm going to do ____," is a basic goal. People instinctively think in the form of goals. We decide what we are going to do. That is the primary goal. Then we plan the steps we must take to get that job done. Those are intermediate goals. Setting goals is an effective way to get things done in the shortest possible time. Time, after all, is our most valuable asset. The more we can accomplish in that time, the better off we are. Goals are very effective time management tools.

Another effective tool is a butter knife. It is a great tool for spreading jelly on bread, but it would be lousy for cutting down a tree. For cutting down trees, you need a powerful chainsaw. To accomplish big things in sales, you need goals that are more like chainsaws than butter knives. For goals that are as powerful as chainsaws, apply the **M.A.C.** principle.

M.A.C. stands for Measurable, Achievable and Challenging. MAC goals provide more focus and faster results. Here is how they work.

Measurable goals must include some action that anyone can easily measure. "I am going to sell 15 magazines today" is a measurable goal. It tells everyone who is going to sell (I am), how many I will sell (15), what will be sold (magazines) and *when* they will be sold (today). "I am going to sell something" is much less measurable and much less effective. Measurable goals allow you to keep track of exactly how well you are doing and keep you focused on reaching your exact goal. Measurability keeps your goals sharp like a chainsaw's cutting chain.

Achievable goals keep us from becoming discouraged and quitting. If you set an <u>impossible</u> goal, you <u>will</u> fail. Nobody likes to fail. Why waste your time trying to reach an impossible goal? Make sure all your goals are achievable so that you can go to work every day with a good chance of success. Achievability keeps us as tough and on-the-job as a chainsaw.

Challenging goals keep us working harder. When you set challenging goals, you set yourself up to outperform yourself (and others.) To set challenging goals, decide how much you can do and then add a little more to it. Challenging goals will drive you to sell more and to make more money. Challenging puts power in our goals like the gas puts power in the chainsaw. Be careful! Gasoline is dangerous, and so are challenging goals. Always balance your goals to make them achievable, as well as challenging. Then you will find yourself routinely surprising others with how much you can accomplish.

This basic concept, a measurable, achievable and challenging goal, may be one of the most important. With great goals, you can do great things!

H is for Honesty

How you can work less and earn more!

Honesty is telling the truth in everything you say. When you consistently tell the truth, people learn to trust you. Customers are always looking for an honest salesperson they can trust. Over time, honesty builds trust. Trust builds positive RELATIONSHIPS. Positive relationships bring your customer back to you to buy more. Honesty usually pays off in repeat business.

Honest salespeople sell more and work less. When you only tell the truth, you only have to remember one story, one set of facts. People who lie are constantly working harder. They must work to remember what story they told to this person and what other story they told to a different person. People who lie are always under stress. They are always worried about someone catching them in their untruths. Who needs that kind of stress on top of the normal workday stress we all feel? After a while, dishonest people must work extra hard to cover their lies as the truth comes out.

Special Note: The Truth Always Comes Out. It may be weeks or years later, but the truth eventually surfaces. If you lie and you are caught, that destroys any trust and any relationship you established with your customers. You may lose their business and may not get it back. Your reputation is tarnished.

That is why honesty is easier. When you always tell the truth, you avoid the stress of deceiving people. What happens if you must deliver bad news to your customers? That causes stress. It certainly does, but the stress of giving customers bad news lasts only a while, then it is over. If, for example, a customer's order will arrive late, it is much better to let them know as soon as possible. They will be disappointed and they may be angry. It would be much worse, however, to wait and let the customer discover the problem as it happens. Telling them the truth early allows them to adjust their plans and work around the problem. Giving customers bad news early shows them that you are more concerned about their order and their business then you are about yourself. It can actually help customers trust you more.

Selling is all about working with people. Since that is true, is it not okay to tell just a little un-truth to keep from hurting someone's feelings? No. Saying nothing is better than lying, and telling the truth may even help that person in the end.

Everyone knows the story of the wife who asks her husband, "Does this dress make me look fat?" (In this case, yes, it does. Trust me. It really does!) If the husband lies and says no, her friends (or worse, a perfect stranger) will say something later that lets her know exactly how fat she looks in that dress. She has her feelings crushed, and it did not have to happen.

Be honest, but not stupid. Just because you discover a problem or an unpleasant fact does not mean you have to broadcast it to the world. Yes, you should always be honest. You should be tactful at the same time. In the example above, the husband could tactfully say, "That dress doesn't make you look nearly as beautiful as you really are. Why don't you wear another one?" Not being stupid, the husband knows there is no reason to insult his wife. He also prevented her from being embarrassed later. Notice that he did not ignore the problem. Avoiding an answer would have resulted in a bad situation, too. He truthfully and tactfully addressed the situation and offered a solution.

Honesty is a key concept of successful selling. Never think that being dishonest or avoiding a customer problem will make your life easier. It will not. Be honest with good news and bad. You will build a trusting relationship between you and all your customers. You will sell more, and enjoy a life with less stress.

I is for Inventory

Everything you have to sell is in your mind.

INVENTORY is the word that describes the group of products (or services) a salesperson has to sell. If you are a salesperson in a shoe store, your inventory is all the sizes and styles of shoes in the store. It is also all the shoelaces, socks, shoe polish and accessories. If you are an insurance salesperson, your inventory is all of the different insurance policies your company offers. If you are a politician running for office, your inventory is all your qualifications, experiences and personality strengths.

Salespeople must be very familiar with their inventory. It does not matter if a company has 200 different products to sell. If the salespeople only know about two of them, only those two products will sell. Salespeople must study the inventory. They must acquire this knowledge to be effective in selling all the products.

The more you know about your products, the easier it is for you to sell them. You can quickly decide which product will best match what your customers want. You must know all the important facts and benefits of your products. Then you can present them in a convincing, enthusiastic way. Your customers can easily see the value in your products, and that is the reason they make a purchase.

Did you know that you can only focus your attention on one thing at a time? You can consider many things in quick succession, but you can only really concentrate on one thing at a time. In selling, always focus your attention on what your customer is saying. If you have to concentrate on remembering things about your inventory (what products do or how much they cost), you will miss something important your customer tells you. Learning your inventory in advance avoids that.

You should know these facts about any product in your inventory:

Who can use it?

What is it used for? What sizes, colors, etc. are available?

When should it be used?

Where should it be used?

How should it be used, and how much does it cost?

Why customers would buy it, not a competitive product?

Restaurant waiters who know their menu make better recommendations, and much bigger tips! Store clerks sell more (and earn more commissions) if they lead customers quickly to products in their stores. As you can see, it really pays to know your inventory well!

Take a break! **Be a Better Buyer!**

When YOU are the customer, buying anything, you can use your understanding of the 26 selling basics in this book to make better purchases. As a buyer, you can understand and predict what salespeople will do. As a buyer, you can grade your salespeople to separate the selling professionals from the amateurs. Everyone would rather work with a professional salesperson who will deliver the service you like, and cares more about what you want than what he wants to sell. As a buyer who understands the basic concepts of selling, you can immediately recognize the best value, and you can tell when the price is right for you. You will never have to suffer through dealings with amateur salespeople again. Now, you can spot an amateur in the first minute, and quietly move on to work with a "Pro" to get the kind of service you give your customers!

Save yourself some valuable time. Do not try to teach these selling basics to salespeople who are trying to sell you something. If they are great salespeople, they already use these basics. If they are not so great, they probably will not be interested in your critique of their efforts (or lack of effort.) If however, you do run across a bright person who you think would really sell better if they knew the basics, please recommend this book to them. Your recommendation will produce at least three benefits.

1) **They will benefit.** As they learn and start using the basic concepts of selling, they will sell more. They will begin to enjoy their work because understanding the basics helps them achieve their sales goals and make more money!

2) **Their customers will benefit.** The basic concepts of selling shift the focus of salespeople from themselves to their customers. Customers are much more comfortable and satisfied with confident salespeople who are great at the basics of selling.

3) **You will benefit** from the good feelings you have when you help someone improve their life. You know the old saying, "Give a man a fish and he can eat for a day. Teach him to fish and he can eat for a lifetime." Selling is like fishing. Give a man a job, and he can work for a day. Teach him to sell, and he can work any day he wants.

Your recommendation creates a win, win, win, situation! OK, break is over. Another basic concept awaits you!

J is for Join

Step into your customer's world.

That is where all the money is!

We each live in our own little world. Salespeople who join their customer's world sell more (and earn more) than self-centered salespeople. Whenever you are around other people, you have two options. You can focus inward, or you can reach outward. In selling, you can focus your attention on yourself, or you can concentrate on your customers, the ones who can buy your products.

Your customers live in their own unique, problem-filled worlds. They are always concerned about getting what they want. They are not concerned about you. They are not concerned about what you are selling. Always keep this in mind when you are working with customers. From a customer viewpoint, the most important thing about your product is - it is not important. What is important is what the customer wants to buy.

Your job as a salesperson is to reach out and join your customers in their current world. The fastest way to do that is to ask customers questions. With questions, you can discover what they want.

You need to be careful and sincere when you ask customers these questions. Trust this; most customers are not spending their day trying to find salespeople to invite into their world! Customers are trying to find whatever it is that they want. They will quickly put up a wall to avoid insincere salespeople who act friendly just to make a sale. You can climb over that wall using the ladder called "Sincerity." Be sincere as you focus on your customer and the problem they wish to solve (or the product they wish to buy.) You will bring that customer good value, and you will be providing the service the customer is seeking. For that, your customer will let you join a part of their world. Here are some good examples of questions that will let you join your customer's world when you talk about products:

    What do you have in mind?

    What do you want this product to do for you?

    Are there any special things you are looking for?

You can also make customers feel more comfortable with you by finding common interests. As you work with the same customers repeatedly, you can build lasting relationships by taking care of their business first, then discovering what else you have in common. It may be a hobby like cars, music or animals. It may be an interest in the same sports team, or you may have mutual friends. As you join their world, you build a valuable relationship with that customer. As you help customers repeatedly, over time they will invite you into more of their world. You eventually become friends. That happens when they decide it should.

If you have ever joined a sports team or the military, you remember that you had to put on their uniform to join. They did not change their uniforms to match the way you looked, did they? Do not expect customers to change in order to join your world, either.

People like to do business with their friends. Use *questions* to find out what your customers want so that they will buy from you today. Use *empathy* to build relationships so that your customer will buy from you tomorrow. Empathy is putting yourself in your customer's place, thinking as they think and wanting what they want. Empathy allows you to get close to your customers. Empathy allows you to join their world. Salespeople with empathy let what the customer wants guide their actions. The first step toward selling with empathy is to pay attention to your customer. Look carefully to determine the customer's mood by watching how they walk, talk, etc. If the customer is happy, you can act happy too. If, however, the customer is obviously having a bad day, the last thing in the world they want is an overly cheery salesperson. Follow the customer's lead to make a positive connection. The connections you make after the first impression are the basis for building a positive relationship. By making positive connections, you will build positive relationships and make friends who will want to buy from you repeatedly. If you make negative impressions, the customer will push you away and you will not make a sale.

How do you make a good connection? Find out what the customer likes. This is easy for outside sales people. They go into customers' offices. Customers' offices are full of clues about what they like. Family photos, diplomas, hobby photos, sports team souvenirs, etc. all show what the customer likes. The best salespeople notice those clues and bring them up in conversation. This shows the customer that the salesperson is interested in them, not just in a sale.

Inside salespeople have fewer clues and often see customers only once. Store clerks and restaurant servers know that it is almost impossible to establish a friendship in one visit. You can, however, make a good first impression and leave a lasting positive impression. Customers will remember you and come back to see you again.

K is for Knowledge

More valuable than gold,

and free for the taking!

Knowledge is critical to successful selling. Sales people who know more about their inventory, customers, TERRITORY, price and competition will sell more (whenever they ask) than salespeople who know less.

There are two reasons for this. One, knowledge gives a salesperson confidence! Two, customer are more comfortable buying from a confident salesperson.

There is good news and bad news about knowledge. Here is the bad news first. The <u>only</u> way you acquire knowledge is by studying. You can learn by watching others, by listening or by reading, but you must actively participate. You have to work at learning. You must give up some of your valuable time to learn something. Now for the good news, and there are two bits of that. First, as you work at learning, you get better at it. As you discover the most effective ways for your brain to learn information, you literally learn how you learn. The more you study, the easier studying becomes for you. Second, gaining knowledge is up to you alone. You decide when, where, and how much you want to learn. You are in charge, and you do not have to wait on anyone's approval to gain knowledge! The knowledge you want is out there and YOU CAN HAVE AS MUCH AS YOU WANT.

Another way to think about knowledge truly demonstrates its value. Knowledge is worth what it costs you *plus* whatever you gain from it. What does knowledge cost you? It costs you your time, obviously. When you spend an hour of your life learning, you can never get that hour back. The richest nation in the world cannot buy back one hour that already passed. Your time is incredibly valuable!

The value of knowledge includes what you can gain from it. You could spend your valuable time goofing off or doing destructive things. You would gain nothing from those activities. Nevertheless, with knowledge, you can create art, build a new business, build a new friendship, sell effectively etc. With knowledge applied effectively with dedication, you can change your life for the better and you can improve the lives of those around you. Second only to time, knowledge is your most valuable asset.

Unlike irreplaceable time, however, you can have as much knowledge as you desire! In addition, knowledge stays with you. Unlike money, gold or gasoline, which are gone as soon as you use them, your knowledge increases as you use it! With knowledge, you are free to change the world around you. Without knowledge, the world is free to change you.

Take a break! **Where has all the knowledge gone?**

Since almost everything on the Earth is bought and sold, you would think that everyone would understand how selling works. Incredibly, selling is a complete mystery to most people. If most high schools and universities taught selling instead of Algebra 2, there would be many more-efficient salespeople and buyers! (Everyone who hated Algebra 2 say Yeah!)

Why do schools very rarely teach selling? Why does the business of buying and selling stumble along inefficiently? The answer to those questions is the fact that **effective selling is too valuable to give away!** Big companies train their salespeople to sell effectively. They spend enormous sums to make their salespeople better than the competition. The return on that investment is more sales and more market share. Do you think those major corporations will sponsor classes in schools to prepare better salespeople for *other* companies? No.

Most small and medium sized businesses do not have the resources to train salespeople well. Those companies make up most of our economy. So, most salespeople learn their selling skills through on-the-job-training (OJT). In other words, they learn as they go. They try, fail and learn from their mistakes. If they cannot learn fast enough, they leave.

Occasionally, individuals figure it out. Somehow, they start applying sales basics. They sell more and earn more for their success. They enjoy the thrill that comes from successful sales. They earn recognition and awards. Many become wealthy through sales. Only a few of these successful salespeople become sales trainers and pass along their knowledge to others. Most successful salespeople keep their knowledge to themselves. Their "how to sell" knowledge gives them a great lifestyle and a lot of money. Why give those valuable secrets away, especially to someone who may compete with them later for a sale?

Something is wrong with a system that lets a few successful people and companies hoard powerful knowledge like this. Everyone should be able to learn how to be more persuasive and sell more. The fact that you are reading this book demonstrates that you agree that this knowledge is valuable enough to share. Please pass it along to other people you know. Recommend this book to others. No one should ever have to be uncomfortable persuading others in the value of a good idea. Education can make all of us more persuasive! Ok, back to the education.

L is for Listening

To sell more, talk less!

Nothing you can tell a customer will let you know what they are willing to buy. Everything a customer tells you can help you sell.

Customers know what they want to buy, and they will tell you. You have to listen. Amazingly, either most salespeople do not know how to listen, or they do not care to listen to customers. Why? It is much easier to recite a memorized sales speech than it is to engage the customer in an actual sales conversation. Another reason is most salespeople are more concerned about themselves and their product than they are concerned about their customers. Salespeople who love to give fact-filled speeches to customers sell less than salespeople who really listen to discover their customers' wants.

The best salespeople do not give sales speeches. They have conversations with customers. They ask questions. They listen intently to their customers' answers. After the customers describe what they want to buy, the salespeople then describe benefits that the customers will receive from their purchases. Benefits sell.

The good news about listening is that anyone who can hear can learn to listen effectively. There is a foolproof system of listening. It is a system, not just a skill, because listening is a set of complex behaviors. Effective listening is much more than not talking.

Have you ever heard of active listening? Active listening is a tool taught in schools and businesses to improve communications. Active listening involves looking at the speaker, not interrupting, focusing your thoughts on what the speaker is saying instead of what you are going to say next, and giving positive feedback signals to let the speaker know you are listening. Good salespeople use active listening. It is a very effective tool. However, there is more to effective listening. The best salespeople take active listening even further. They use the three-steps of a more effective listening process: **Complete Listening**.

>Step One: **Proactive** Listening

>Step Two: **Interactive** Listening

>Step Three: **Reactive** Listening

The first step in Complete Listening is **Proactive Listening**. Proactive Listening is *preparing to listen*. Drop what you are doing, clear your mind of everything else and focus your attention on what the customer is going to say next. Turn your body towards the customer and look completely focused on them. (You would not throw a ball to someone who was not looking at you, ready to catch it. Why would someone throw information to you if you were not looking at him or her, ready to hear it?)

The second step of Complete Listening is **Interactive Listening**. Interactive Listening is *receiving the information*. It is truly active listening. Focus your thoughts on receiving their information. Look at the speaker. Lean in slightly and nod occasionally to show your interest. Give occasional positive feedback to show the speaker you are receiving their message. Take notes, if it is appropriate. Ask questions to clarify your understanding, but only if you really need to ask. Do not ask questions to take over the conversation. With Interactive Listening, you really focus on learning what the other people have to say. They will tell you exactly what they want to buy.

The third step in Complete Listening is **Reactive Listening**. Reactive listening is *analyzing and processing the important information* the customer just gave you. Is it important? Yes! All information from customers is important. Some information is more important because it helps you sell your product right now, but all of it is important. Customers may tell you something you can use later, so keep good records. Take notes, and file the information you decide is most important. As soon as you can, plan your next step to sell that customer something else. Based upon what you have learned, decide what your next sales action should be. Plan when you should do it, and enter the actions on your calendar.

Reactive Listening is new to most salespeople. It is the step between customer contact and your follow-up. Inside salespeople can use Reactive Listening every day. It happens in a few seconds, during your conversation with a walk-in customer. The customer gives you information, and you have a few seconds to evaluate the customer's wants and then show the customer your product that best suits them.

Reactive Listening could also take hours, following a first outside sales visit on a potential new corporate customer. Large corporate deals may take weeks or months to win, so you do not want to lose any time by not capturing the important information the customer gave you. The fastest way to make a sale is to react the right way to all the information that a customer provides.

One of the fastest ways to lose a sale is to lose information. Customers remember what they tell you. If you do not care enough about them to listen and to remember what they said, why should they buy from you?

A special listening challenge is the angry customer. Everyone eventually has an out-of-control angry customer. Think of that customer as a hurricane. They are going to blow, and nothing you can do can stop them. So do not try. A hurricane can blow over the strongest tree, and an angry customer can blow over any strong-willed salesperson. The key to surviving the onslaught is flexibility. Bend in the wind! Let them vent. Right or wrong, they feel so strongly in that moment that they simply must vent their feelings. It is just too bad that you are the nearest salesperson at the time!

In this situation, remain in a neutral non-combative attitude. Listen attentively without smiling or frowning. Take an interest in their position, but do not take a hard position of your own, either for or against them. After they have "blown off some steam" and they seem ready for a two-way conversation, tell them you understand how they might feel that way. (That is not the same thing as telling them they are right.)

If you have listened well, you will know what the customer wants. If it is justified, and if it is in your power to grant that, go ahead. If it is not in your power, then your best move is to seek help from your manager. If you are your own manager, it is still a good idea to tell the customer you will get back to them after you have investigated the matter. Most of the time, you do not have to make an on-the-spot decision. If you are human, listening to an angry customer makes you a little upset. That is okay and normal. You will make a better decision after you have had time to cool down and think about what is best for your business.

The old adage, "The customer is always right," really means, "The customer always wins a fight." It never pays to fight with an angry customer. You both lose, and the customer might spend years creating and spreading wild stories about your company's horrible service.

Take a break! **Train your brain!**

You trust yourself more than you trust any other person. If you tell yourself something, you tend to believe it. If you tell yourself something enough times, you <u>will</u> believe it. This is a form of self-hypnosis, and it can be a very powerful force in your life. In college as I studied psychology, we experimented with a particular type of mental programming. The purpose of the experiment was to "train our brains," to program them to do something subconsciously without our consciously thinking about it. We wrote down short rhymes that contained a positive idea and an action phrase. The positive idea was there as "bait" to make the rhyme appealing to our subconscious. The action phrase contained a measurable activity. It contained the elements: who, what, and where. It was something we would consciously recognize if it worked.

My programming rhyme was, "I'm the luckiest man I know, I find money everywhere I go, just lying around in the street." I wrote that idea down and read it aloud dozens of time a day for several weeks. Can you guess what happened? I began to find money: pennies, nickels, dimes, quarters, even dollar bills! Other people walked right over them, but my subconscious brain spotted them for me. Thirty years later, I still reinforce that idea, and I still find money in the street almost every day. It is a lot of fun.

You can train your brain to think positively, to lose weight, to stop smoking, etc. If you are interested in this topic, search for self-hypnosis on the web. That will provide you with a large source of books and sites to investigate. This break is over. Turn the page to start learning more about your next basic concept.

M is for More

Everybody wants more, and you can give it to them!

Everybody wants more. We all want to feel like we got the better part of any deal. We always want to get the best value for the price we had to pay. Customers who believe they received more when they purchased from someone usually do two things:

    They brag to their friends about their deal.

    They come back to buy again.

Many restaurants in the United States understand this "more" concept very well. They serve you more food than you can possibly eat. The servers keep refilling your drink glass, too. This "extra" service does not cost the restaurant very much, but it makes a big impression on the customers. Those customers usually brag to their friends about the great deal they got, and they come back to that restaurant to eat again!

Many clothing stores offer free alterations for one year on any clothes you buy. Most people do not change size much, and most people who do will not bother getting clothes altered. Those stores make customers happy by offering more, the free alteration service. In this case, it is free to the store as well, if nobody uses it. Another example of this is a free towing service if your new car breaks down. Since most new cars do not break down, this service costs the car dealer very little. The lesson here is this. You do not have to give anything away to satisfy the customer's desire for more.

Whatever you are selling, find a way to give your customer more. Even if it is just a tiny thing, your customer will appreciate getting more. For example, after you sell a shirt, show the customer the spare button that is sewn onto the hem. After you sell someone a hamburger and fries, drop a few extra fries into their to-go bag. After you sell a car, tell the customer they can bring it back for a free car wash. All of these examples will pay for themselves by the free word-of-mouth advertising you receive as your customers happily brag to their friends about the good deal they made. You give them a chance to look smart to their peers for their shrewd shopping. Besides that, they will be much more likely to come back and buy from you again.

A simple way to give your customer more is to always promise less and deliver more. Whenever you can, promise your customer a service that you know you can improve upon. For example, promise your customer delivery that is later than you know you can provide. Most customers will be happy when you can deliver their product "early."

Caution: always, always, promise less and deliver more, not the other way around! If you promise *more* but deliver *less*, be ready for your customer to have a wonderful time telling horror stories about your poor service to anyone who will listen to them. People *like* to tell others about a good deal they made, but they *love* to tell horror stories about poor service. People are like that.

This basic concept teaches us effort affects sales. The more effort you put into your selling, the more sales you will make. It takes additional effort on your part to think of ways to give your customers greater service. It would take less work to coast along, selling like everyone else. That little extra effort, however, can come back to you in many additional sales. Put sticky notes with the word "MORE" on the dashboard of your car and on your bathroom mirror to remind you to start doing more (and selling more!) It takes 21 days to form a new habit, so in just three weeks, you can form the habit of doing more for your customers. Try this concept soon. You will see results right away.

N is for No

No means "Ask me why."

"No" is the most important word in selling. Without the word no, there is no need for salespeople! Businesses would only need order-takers to service all the customers lined up waiting to buy. Be thankful for the word no.

Salespeople understand that all selling begins with the customer thinking no. No is people's natural state of mind. No protects us from buying things we do not need and from doing things we do not want to do. No puts us in charge. A 2-year old can take charge of two adult parents by simply saying "No!" and refusing to eat. After a while, the parents will do anything to get the child to eat.

When your customer says no, they think, "I do not believe the value of your product is worth the price." It is nothing personal. Customers will naturally think no until they believe the product has enough value to make them want it. <u>Then</u> they buy.

You persuade customers to say yes by explaining enough benefits so the customer believes the product has value. Every sale follows the same format. Customers begin the buying process saying no to every product. As they begin to realize that they have a problem to solve, they begin to want some item. When they really want to solve that problem or obtain that item, they start to shop around until they see a product that attracts them with the benefits it offers. They compare items, and when they discover a product that has more than enough benefits to outweigh the price, they buy it. The more benefits a product offers the more value the customer sees in it. Until they believe the value of the product is worth the price, customers will say no to buying anything.

There are hundreds of ways for customers to say no. Some of them are:

Not today.

Maybe later.

It is not my size.

It costs too much.

I do not have time.

It is the wrong color.

It makes me look fat.

Let me think about it.

Call me back tomorrow.

My wife will not like it.

> This is not a good time.
>
> Yes, okay. (What a liar!)
>
> I am going to shop around first.
>
> Can you give me a better deal?
>
> (And the particularly effective), "That sounds good. Why don't you check back with me in a few weeks?"

There are just as many reasons *why* a customer would say no. Customers say no if your product is not useful to them. Either they do not have a problem your product can solve, or they do not believe your product is able to solve a problem they have. In order to persuade them to say yes, you need to discover the exact reason they are not buying. Once you know that reason, you can address it specifically. **It is your right and your responsibility to ask a customer why they say no.**

Just as polite people naturally say, "Bless you," after someone sneezes, salespeople should naturally ask "Why?" after a customer says no. I recommend that you do not loudly blurt out, "Why?" That word, used alone, can come across as pushy or aggressive. It is much more effective to use a softer, conversational tone. Your goal is to keep the conversation going in order to discover the real reason behind the no.

Here are many non-threatening, easy ways to ask why. Make sure you smile as you ask your brief question.

>"May I please ask why?"
>
>"Oh? What makes you say that?"
>
>"Will you please share your reason for that?"
>
>"Is there a particular reason why?"
>
>"Why you would say that?

The point of all these questions is to learn the customer's real reason for not buying. When the customer shares the reason for not buying, then it is your turn to talk. Never argue. To make the sale, you have to help the customer see enough value in what you are selling so that they want to buy it. You can read how to do that in the chapters on value and want.

Take a break! **Plastic combs, drugs and keys.**

I stunk on my first job as a salesperson. When my high school band director asked us to sell packages of plastic combs for a fundraiser, I froze. Other band kids had no problem going door-to-door selling those combs. Not me, I avoided it as long as I could and sold just enough to get by. The problem was that I thought about it too much. I did not know how to sell, so I avoided it. That was strange, because I was a persuasive person. I had no problem "selling" my ideas to my family and friends. I did not know what to say to customers, and I was afraid that people would say no. (Of course, they would! Everyone thinks and says no until you show them the benefits of what you are selling.) If I knew then how selling worked, I would have been OK with that and I would have sold a hundred of those plastic combs!

Years later, after college and time in the Army, I applied for sales jobs. Research told me the fastest way into corporate management was through sales. A large pharmaceutical firm hired me because I had enthusiasm, Army self-discipline and extensive chemical weapons knowledge. To them, that meant I understood biochemistry.

For five 16-hour days, my manager and a trainer tag-teamed trained me. They explained precisely how the job worked: who to see, what to say, where to go, and when to see the doctors. At night, I studied our drugs and the competition. I memorized the information and passed all their tests. I asked tons of "what-if" questions, and they answered them all.

On the afternoon of the last day, I was ready to start my new sales career. The manager told me to drive him to the airport and to stop along the way to make my very first sales call.

I was confident, and so serious (and a little nervous), as I parked the car at the doctor's office. The manager went in with me, and the sales call went just as we trained! I presented the products, and the doctor said he would definitely use them for his patients. My manager just smiled the whole time.

I felt wonderful! As we left the office, my manager asked a question I still remember whenever I am making sales calls. "Dale, how are you planning to get your keys out of the car?" I had locked my keys in the car! My manager had seen me do it, and that is why he had been smiling! He thought it was hilarious! Anyway, I sheepishly got the car unlocked and made it to the airport in time for his flight.

What a difference between the high school kid who would not sell plastic combs and the professional pharmaceutical salesperson! My new understanding of sales made the very positive difference. I hope that this book will help you understand sales, so you can enjoy selling, too. Perhaps it will even save you from locking your keys in the car! Ok, back to the basics.

O is for Organization

Teamwork for one!

Everyone knows the value of teamwork. Teamwork focuses the efforts of a group into a single powerful force. What teamwork does for a group, ORGANIZATION does for an individual. Organization focuses the efforts of any individual into a single powerful force.

Organization allows you to accomplish more in your day. The number one trait of award-winning salespeople is not a pleasant personality. It is not a pretty face. It is not good communication skills. In over 20 years of professional selling, I have seen thousands of mediocre salespeople with those traits. The number one trait of top selling, award-winning salespeople is organization! They simply do more and make more sales.

Imagine two outside salespeople. They have identical inventories and similar territories. They both work eight full hours a day. Salesperson Number 1 organizes his work to make ten productive sales calls each

An important part of being organized is doing paperwork. Here are a few important words about paperwork. Every sales job requires some sort of paperwork, and nearly every salesperson would rather sell than fill out that paperwork. That is just the way we are! However, paperwork is not a four-letter word, and it is not your enemy.

As a young salesperson, I avoided paperwork, until I discovered this valuable selling truth - paperwork works for you, not the other way around. Here is the value of paperwork for any salesperson. First, **paperwork gets you paid!** If your sale orders or ships incorrectly, you will not get your reward for that sale. Second, **paperwork gets you promoted.** Managers do not spend much time with you as a salesperson. Managers do spend a lot of time with your paperwork.

Think of paperwork as your ambassador to management. No matter how much you sell, your managers, all the way to the top, regularly see your paperwork, not you. Either your paperwork impresses them with accuracy, neatness and timeliness, or it does not. Which salespeople will the managers choose when a special opportunity or promotion becomes available? They usually consider salespeople who successfully sell *and* submit quality paperwork. The time you invest to submit accurate, neat and on-time paperwork is always worthwhile!

P is for Price

The price is right only on TV game shows.

For customers, it always starts too high.

Price is what a customer agrees to pay for your product. Prices can be negotiable or locked-in. An example of locked-in pricing is a snack vending machine. The price shows under the snack, and you buy it or not. Negotiable pricing, on the other hand, allows the seller and the customer to agree on a best price, as when someone buys a house.

Every price is too high for *every* customer in the beginning of *every* sale. Consider that vending machine. People walk by it all day long without purchasing a snack because the price is too high for people who are not hungry. When someone gets hungry enough, suddenly the price is right. Then they buy from the machine.

All sales work the same way. Until customers believe that the product has enough value, they will not want it. When they do not want

P is for Price

it, every price is too high. The main job of salespeople is to convince customers that the product has enough value to be worth the price. A sale happens when the customer agrees that the price is not too high.

The sale price can be very high if the customer wants the product enough. If the customer's want for the product is low, the price must be low to make the sale. Real estate provides some great examples. Hundreds of people can look at the same house, and only a few will want it at the selling price. Normally, when people do want the house enough, they make a serious, but low offer to buy it. The seller can accept that offer or come back with a price that is lower than the original but higher than the buyer's offer. This is negotiation, and it goes back and forth until the buyer and seller agree on a price. Then the house sells.

A different example is a gas station. The gas station owner wants to sell gasoline, so he opens his station and turned on his pumps. He puts up signs to attract customers who are driving by. Customers drive by, and the ones who agree that his price is OK will stop. They turn in and fill up their tanks. The gasoline sells, and the gas station owner makes a profit on the sale.

What is a profit? Profit is the money you make when you sell something for more than it cost you to buy it, or make it. People sell things to make a profit. In the real estate example, the seller made a profit if the selling price was more than what he paid for the house *plus* his expense of selling it. No law says you must sell your product for a profit. Companies however, must make profits or run out of money and go out of business. No law says customers must pay any price a seller asks. The higher your price, the more value you must show, otherwise, no customers will pay that high a price for what you are selling.

There are two kinds of prices, asking and selling. The asking price is how much money the seller wants to receive for the product. The selling price is the amount of money a customer will actually pay for the product. The more a product costs, the more a seller will usually reduce the asking price to make the sale. In business, coming to an agreement between the asking price and selling price is negotiation, or bargaining.

Sellers and buyers negotiate together to agree on a price. Here is an example of a basic negotiation. Randy has a car for sale. His asking price is $12,000. A buyer offers Randy $10,000 for the car. Randy says no and counter offers $11,500. The buyer wants the car, and counter offers $10, 500. Randy wants to sell the car, so he counters with $11,000. The buyer agrees and they have a deal.

Negotiating is an art. If you want to be good at negotiating, read books, study and practice. With study and practice, anyone can learn to be a skilled negotiator.

Take a break! **An American Disadvantage**

Americans are at a distinct disadvantage to citizens of other countries where bargaining is the norm. In much of the world, consumers bargain for their everyday purchases. In markets all over the world, the seller expects a buyer to bargain for a lower price. Americans evolved from bargaining into the "supermarket mentality." That means the price marked on a product is final. In supermarkets, the seller is all-powerful, and the buyer must "take it or leave it." How exquisitely arrogant!

Sellers get away with this business model because buyers have enough money, but not enough time. Americans will pay more for variety and convenience. The supermarket system fits our fast paced, affluent lifestyle, but it kills our negotiating skills. Americans have become buyers, not sellers

Most Americans, because they are unused to selling or bargaining, stress out when they see themselves placed in a selling situation. This is really just a perception problem, because most of us "sell" everyday. Selling is simply persuading others that your idea has value. If everyone understood the basic concepts of selling, they could avoid much of that stress and enjoy selling!

Q is for Questions

Questions are the keys that unlock sales.

All sales begin with customers thinking no, and it is up to salespeople to move the customers' thinking toward yes. Only customers know exactly what they want. Questions are the keys you use to open up customers, to help them describe what they want to buy. When you know what they want, you can show them how your product matches that description.

Questions are also the tools you use to ask customers to buy your product, or give you other information. Like any tools, there are many types. You become skilled at using them by practicing with them.

There are two basic types of questions: short answer questions and long answer questions. The short answer questions require just a word or two in answer: yes or no, a number, a color, etc. Salespeople use short answer questions to direct a customer's attention to a certain fact.

These are examples of short answer quesitons:

    Do you like cookies? (Yes or no.)

    How many cookies do you eat at once? (A number.)

    Would you like to buy two cookies or three?

Short answer questions give the customer only a few options for an answer. Since you can be ready to respond to any of the possible short answers, short answers give you control over conversations.

Long answer questions open up the conversation. Long answer questions give the customer permission to talk more and to share their thoughts. You use long answer questions to get information that helps you join the customer's world and discover what the customer wants. Examples:

    What do you like about cookies?

    What is good about your favorite cookie?

    Why do you think people love cookies?

As you have already guessed, the point of all questions is to sell cookies. No matter what you are selling, be prepared to listen carefully after you ask a question. The information the customer gives you is like gold. It is valuable insight into what the customer believes. Once you know more about what your customer believes and wants, then you can tell that customer how your product can really benefit them.

Alphabetical Basic Concepts of SELLING

Customers will tell you exactly what they want to buy, *if* you give them the chance. Ask good questions to get them talking. If the customer talks 50% of the time, and you talk 50% of the time then you have a 50% chance of making the sale. If they talk 75% of the time, you have an even better chance of making the sale. On the other hand, if you talk 100% of the time, your chances of selling anything go down to zero (how can a customer say yes if you're doing all the talking!)

Why is this true? Customers care more about what they want to buy than what you want to sell. This idea is so important is that I am going to repeat it again. Customers care more about what they want to buy than what you want to sell.

"Pushy" salespeople never let a customer say much, and customers do not like that. It makes them feel uncomfortable. On the other hand, what makes customers feel comfortable is the sound of their own voice. The more they talk in a conversation with you, the more comfortable they will feel with you. This makes them more likely to buy from you.

Learn to ask good questions to keep the customer talking about what they want. You can easily fit your product benefits into the two-way conversation. Customers enjoy talking to (and buying from) salespeople who always listen to their customers carefully. You should ask one very

Q is for Questions

important question in every sale. That question is some version of,

"Will you please buy this product from me today?"

It is your job as a salesperson to ask them for their business. It is your job as a salesperson to close your presentation by asking them to buy your product. That is why asking them to buy is closing the sale.

If you do not specifically ask every customer to buy from you, you will miss many sales. Customers might love your product but decide to buy it from someone else. They might agree that they want what you are selling, but just not right now. To sell effectively, specifically ask each customer to buy what you are selling. It makes sense to close each sales presentation by asking for their business. Here are some poor, good and better examples of how to ask customers to buy your product. First, some poor examples:

You don't want to buy any ____ today, do you?

(Of course, they don't if you ask like that.)

So, what do you think? (About what?)

Here are some good examples:

Would you please buy one of these today?

Do you want to buy one now?

Here are some better examples:

>Shall I order one of these for you now?

>Which one of these ___ will you buy today?

>How would you like to pay for these today?

>Would you like to buy this one, or that one?

Your closing question should always make it convenient for the customer to buy from you. Offering customers a choice is a good way to make the customer feel like they are in charge of the sale. Instead of asking if the customer wants to buy, ask the customer if they want to buy this one or that one, A or B, chocolate or vanilla, etc. They get a choice, and you make a sale!

Another important question to ask is, "How will you be paying for this today?" The sale really is not over until the customer has paid you. Keep that in mind. Do not spend your valuable time selling to customers who cannot or will not pay you the correct amount on time. In many sales, customers order your product and agree to pay you later. Never be embarrassed or afraid to go back to that customer to collect your money. Asking a customer to pay what they owe is basic business, and the customer expects you to call on them to collect. In fact, most customers simply wait to pay until the salesperson calls to collect.

You are doing them a favor by reminding them what they owe. When you call them to collect, smile and simply say that you need to get their payment for the last order. These days, most businesses will quickly give you a credit card number, a check or cash to pay for their order.

Always respect your customers by asking them directly if they would like to buy your product or service. They deserve that respect because they are giving you something valuable. At the same time, when you give them something valuable in return, you make a sale and you are helping the economy of your city, county, state, country and the world! Be proud to ask them to buy your product

Another excellent question to use on every sales call is, "Do you know of anyone else who might want to buy one of these?" This question is a "referral." Referrals are recommendations from a customer of other people who might buy your product. Referrals are usually very good sales leads. Your customer will have a good idea of who might really want your product. In addition, when you can tell the referral that your first customer sent you, you have credibility. Asking for referrals is the best way to find new customers. It takes you to seconds to ask a question, and it saves you hours of prospecting to find another new customer.

R is for Relationships

People like to do business with their friends.

Good selling will produce a sale the first time. Good relationships will produce sales the second, third, fourth, etc. times. As you develop a good relationship with your customers, you will find it easier and easier to sell to them. If you fall into a bad relationship, it will be very difficult to sell them anything.

Relationships take shape over time, and it is the salesperson's job to begin the process. When you see your customers for the first time, expect them to hide behind a wall of indifference. Why should they care about you or what you have to sell? You cannot blame them. As we mentioned in "J is for Join," customers expect some salespeople to fake friendliness just long enough to take advantage of people. You will have to show them that you are different.

You show customers that you are different by using the three B's of good relationships: Be sincere. Be honest. Be there.

1) Be sincere. Start good relationships by sincerely caring about your customers and helping them solve their problems. Customers can see right through fake sincerity, so you have to keep it real. Put what they want ahead of what you want to sell them and they will respect you for your sincerity.

2) Be honest. Honesty is the glue that holds relationships together. You must be completely honest with your customers. As customers learn that you are an honest and truthful salesperson, they will begin to trust you. Customers are always looking for a salesperson they can trust. After a while, customers will realize that they trust you, and that you care about their wants. That is the basis of a good relationship. To make that relationship strong and lasting, you have to be there when they need you, and that is the third B.

3) Be there. Customers will feel comfortable with you when they believe they can depend upon you for good service. They need to know you will be there to help them when they call. You accomplish is by working a regular schedule. Let your customers know what hours you

work. Give them your phone number and e-mail so that they can contact you. Make yourself convenient to work with, and people will want to buy from you.

The best salespeople contact their customers on a regular basis, whether the customers need to buy something or not. The contacts you make in between your sales are valuable for relationship building. Every time you see your customers, learn something new about them. As you get to know them better, they get to know you better, and your relationship grows. Your customers will see that you do indeed care about them and their business. Many salespeople develop friendships with customers that last for years or even a lifetime.

Good strong relationships will overcome problems. That is important because all businesses have problems. Maybe a product delivery is late, or maybe your product is defective. If you have a good relationship with your customers, they will work with you as you solve those problems instead of buying from someone else.

Here is some great news. When competing salespeople try to cut into your sales by calling on your customer/friends, they will hit the same wall of indifference you experienced at first. You however, with your solid relationships with your customers, are now standing on top of that wall smiling down on all those other competing salespeople!

Take a break! **Success is a social event.**

Selling requires at last two people, a seller and a customer. Success in selling requires customers, and it usually requires many of them. Since people like to do business with their friends, decide right now that you will learn how to make friends, and keep in contact with those friends.

They say in business, it is not who you know, buy who knows you that matters. Start making as many friends in as many places as you can. These are not customers, yet. Friends help you through losses and help you celebrate wins. Join groups, meet your neighbors, and invest some time making friends! There are many professional groups, church groups, civic groups, hobby groups etc. that will always welcome new members. Visit some of these groups to see if you like the people there. There is no obligation to join if you are just visiting. You might make some friends.

Like most of the alphabetical basic concepts of selling, making friends is a topic about which there are thousands of books. It is a good investment of your time to study the art of making friends.

Here is a tip to help you quickly make new friends. Whenever you are in a social situation, like a business reception or at church, take the first step to meet someone. Walk up to someone you do not know, *smile* and say, "I have not met you yet. My name is _____, and I just wanted to say hello." Offering your hand for a handshake might leave you standing with your hand out (if the other person does not take it), so just smile and speak. You will be amazed at how many people will enter into a friendly conversation with you if you start it first.

Friends enrich your life in many areas besides business. When you build good relationships with people, your life is more interesting. You feel connected to your friends. They feel connected to you, as well. Isolation, not healthy connections to a broad circle of friends, is often associated with depression. Friends keep you mentally healthy (and you can rely on them to tell you when you have spinach stuck in the front of your teeth!)

OK, the break is over. It is time to learn another basic concept.

S is for Service

Take good care of your customers,

and they will take care of you!

Service is all the things you do for your customers before and after they do only one thing for you – buy your product. The amount of service you need to provide depends on how much your customer wants your product. If they absolutely must have your product, you can provide less service. Gas stations, for example, provide no service whatsoever. You need gas to be able to drive your car, so you buy gas.

On the other hand, when customers buy things they want but do not absolutely need, service becomes important. Luxury items like fine jewelry, exclusive dining, high fashion clothing and expensive cars are good examples. Shoppers of luxury items demand good service, and they decide where to spend their large amounts of money based upon the quality and quantity of service they receive.

Before a sale happens, you can impress customers with how you professionally serve them. Customers appreciate a salesperson that sincerely cares about them. Customers appreciate salespeople who do not waste time, who know the answers to questions, and who can make the sale without mistakes in billing, delivery, etc. Importantly, customers appreciate a salesperson with a pleasant attitude, someone who seems very happy to provide service to their customer. Who would want to buy anything from a grump?

Some examples of after-the-sale service are free installation for kitchen appliances, free delivery for furniture, free gift-wrapping for presents, free maintenance for automobiles, free cleaning for jewelry and free sharpening for knives. A guarantee is a form of service, and it is important to many customers. If the product breaks while it still guaranteed, the customer expects the service of a quick repair.

The best way to provide excellent service for your customer is to keep asking yourself, "If I was the customer, how would I want to be treated?" If you are not certain about how to provide excellent service, ask other successful salespeople how they do it. Watch them and learn. As you imitate what they do for customers, you will see how your customers react. From that reaction, you will learn the best services you can provide to help your sales grow.

Here is a basic service anyone can do immediately. Thank your customers. Thank them for shopping with you whether they buy anything or not. Especially thank them when they buy something. Anyone spending his or her time and hard-earned money with you deserves a pleasant, sincere thank you. Do you agree?

SPECIAL NOTE TO READERS:

"**Thank you** for buying and reading this book! I appreciate you."

                                                            From Dale

Always practice what you teach!

T is for Territory

All your present and future customers

together in one tidy package.

Territory is the term used to describe all of your customers and your potential customers. If you are an outside salesperson, your territory may be a zip code, or a city, or a state, or an entire country. An inside sales person might have one department in a store, or maybe just one counter in a department as a territory. Regardless of the size of your territory, it consists of individual customers. As you know from reading this book, it is your job as a salesperson to join your customers' worlds, ask questions to identify what your customers want, share the benefits of your product so that your customers can see the value and ask them to buy. Of course, you provide outstanding service before and after the sale to build a good relationship and sell more. See how these basic concepts fit together?

Organization is the key to making your territory a productive business. Organization helps both outside salespeople and inside salespeople produce more sales from a typical day of selling.

If you are an outside salesperson, learn where your customers are located and when is the best time for them to see you. Plan a way to see as many customers in a day as possible. Doesn't it make sense that if you can make more good selling presentations, you will make more sales? Driving back and forth across a large territory will reduce the number of calls you can make in a day. It is better to stay in one part of the territory all day instead of losing time driving back and forth. (I know of some salespeople who make sales calls with their cell phones while they are driving. I also know salespeople who have wrecked their cars while using cell phones! Please do not sell and drive at the same time.)

If you are an inside sales person, organization can allow you work with more customers each day. A telephone salesperson will make more calls per hour if he is well organized. Of course, the more calls you make the more you sell. Sales clerks in stores will be able to help more customers per hour if they know what merchandise is available to sell and where it is located. They will quickly direct customers to the products they want to buy, make the sale and move on to the next customer with a cheery, "Hello, how may I help you today?"

Inside or out, always be looking for new business from your territory. Own your territory. Work every part of it, whether your territory includes three states or three counters in a store. If you are not assigned a specific territory, you are one lucky salesperson! If you can call on anyone anywhere to sell your products, the only thing holding you back is how much time you can work each day.

Take a break! **Sales: hot, warm and cold**

Outside sales is the opposite of inside sales. Clerks in stores wait for customers to come inside the store to buy. That is inside sales. Outside salespeople go to the customers, instead of the customers coming to them.

In outside sales, a tip that a customer wants to buy something is a sales lead (pronounced leed.) If that information will absolutely lead you to a sale, it is a hot lead. An example of a hot lead is a customer leaving a message wanting to place an order. A tip that *might* result in a sale is a warm lead. A customer calling for information about your product is a warm lead. A cold lead is really no tip at all.

A sales call is anytime you go see a customer in order to sell something. Most salespeople think of a sales call as a face-to-face visit with a customer. A telephone conversation can also be a sales call, but it will not be as effective as a face-to-face-meeting. You cannot read the body language or the facial expressions of customers on a telephone call.

There is another thing about telephone calls. Many customers find it easier to say no on the phone than in person. If you can make your selling presentation in person, be there.

Salespeople rate sales calls the same way as sales leads. If you already know a customer is going to buy, it is a hot call. If you can reasonably expect the customer to buy, it is a warm call. If you have not seen the customer before, and you do not even have an appointment, it is a cold call. Hot leads and calls result in more sales than warm ones. Warm leads and calls sell more than cold ones.

Cold calling on new customers is one of the most enjoyable parts of any sales job, *IF* you do it correctly. As you enter your customer's business, remember that you are *in their world* and *on their time*. Both are very valuable to the customer. The first thing you must do is introduce yourself to the first person you see. Explain who you are and what business you represent. Then you must give that person a one sentence great reason to let you speak with the buyer. The first person you see is the "gate-keeper." They decide to let you see whoever can buy your product. Treat all gatekeepers with respect and patience as you wait to see the buyer. When you see the buyer, make a great first impression and start your sales call well.

OK. It is time to go back for more basics.

.

U is for Up Selling

Do you want fries with that?

Up selling is asking a customer to buy just a little more. More what? More of whatever you are selling. The fast food industry made up selling famous when someone very brilliant began asking everyone who ordered a hamburger, "Do you want fries with that?" To most customers, fries made sense with a hamburger, so they said yes. Many hamburger places have had wonderful success up selling fries and drinks. These days, before you even begin to order, many fast food places ask you if you want to try a combination meal.

Up selling works well because your customers have already decided to buy. They believe that they can trust you and that your product has value. They are going to spend their money with you. What a perfect time to offer them something else they might want! This is one of the easiest ways to increase your total sale. All the customer needs to do is spend just a little more.

U is for Up Selling

Here are some examples of good up selling opportunities.

- a new shirt and tie when the customer has bought a business suit
- ear rings with a new necklace
- a new belt with a new pair of pants
- new socks with new shoes
- a radio upgrade with a new car
- an additional warranty with a new anything
- popcorn when you go to see a movie

Speaking of movies, video rental stores have embraced the up sell concept beautifully. When you check out, you can buy candy, popcorn, gift cards, etc. They will also ask you (and this is The Best!) if you want to buy damage protection insurance for an additional 25 cents. What a great up sell! It costs them nothing to ask you this question, but by asking everyone, they rake in thousands of quarters!

The key to successful up selling is asking everyone. As soon as your customer agrees to buy your product or service, ask them, "Would you like _____ to go with that?" Many of the customers you ask will say no. Some of the customers you ask will say yes, however, and they will add significantly to your sales.

Take a break! **The champion of up selling!**

One of the most famous examples of a successful up sell is from American history. In April 1803, President Thomas Jefferson of the new United States was trying to buy the Port of New Orleans from Emperor Napoleon Bonaparte of France. Jefferson sent James Monroe and Robert Livingston to see Napoleon to make the purchase. Jefferson was prepared to spend up to 10 million dollars for the Port of New Orleans.

At that time, Napoleon seriously needed cash. He did not need 530 million acres of American wilderness. Napoleon, in a flash of selling brilliance, planned what may be the biggest up sell in history. Napoleon sold New Orleans to the Americans on the condition that they must accept a special deal. For just a little more, they could also buy all the land from New Orleans to what is now Canada! President Jefferson had not intended to buy so much land, but he agreed to pay three cents an acre, or 15 million dollars, for all of what they called the Louisiana Purchase. In those days, that was not cheap, but it made sense to Jefferson to spend more and expand his country. That was a nice up sell, Napoleon!

V is for Value

One good thing is a benefit,

The sum of all good things is the value.

As you will remember, a benefit is *one* good thing the customer believes your product or service can do for them. *Value is the total of all the benefits your customer believes.* In other words, value is the sum of all the good things customers believe your product will do for them. Customers come to believe in one benefit at a time, adding to the value. When the value of what you are selling outweighs the price, the customer will buy.

The sales scale on the next page shows how, at the beginning of any sale, the price always outweighs the value in the customer's mind. Before any sale happens, the customer must begin to believe in the benefits of your product. As benefits add up, value outweighs the price and the sale happens. However, as you learned in the price chapter, every price is initially too much.

This sales scale shows how every sale works. With the scale tipped toward No, the customer does not believe the product has value. The price is too great. There is no way he/she will consider buying it.

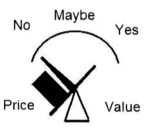

This is the normal state of mind for a customer who has no need or does not want this product now. When, however, the customer develops a need or begins to want the product, then the value begins to outweigh the price. As the value increases, the sales scale will tip towards yes. Now the customer is in the "Maybe" state of mind.

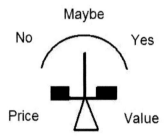

Selling is persuading the customer that your product has enough value to outweigh the price. You add value by explaining one benefit at a time. When your customer believes that benefit, they move closer to saying yes and buying your product. When the benefits add up to enough value, the sales scale tips toward Yes, and the sale happens.

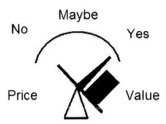

Want and benefits are closely related. The more benefits the customer believes your product has, the more your customer will want your product. The key to selling is explaining enough benefits so that the customer sees sufficient value to outweigh the price.

Sometimes customers believe in a product's value before they talk to a salesperson. Those customers are ready to buy right now. It is very important for you, the salesperson, to recognize that situation when it happens and make the sale immediately! You can easily talk customers out of buying. You might mention some issue that bothers the customer enough to stop the sale. That is like subtracting benefits from the value. If that ever happens to you, save your sale by adding more benefits. There is no need for you to continue selling once a customer says yes they are ready to buy. Close that sale quickly.

Take a break! **When 10% means 1.1 Billion Dollars!**

"Selling" plays an important part in everyone's life. We "sell" other people on agreeing with our ideas in our daily conversations. Everybody sells. What is the difference between selling an idea and selling a product? There is no difference.

When you use the basic concepts of selling, your sales increase because you spend your time doing more of the important things that make sales happen. How much will your sales increase? 10%, 200% or more? It all depends on how many of the basics you were using before.

Imagine how much stronger your company would be, or the economy of our country would be if all the salespeople suddenly became 10% more efficient. In 2005, the United States recorded a Gross National Product of $11.059 trillion. The GNP is the total value of all final goods and services produced by a country's factors of production and **sold** on the market in a given time period. If all the salespeople in the United States suddenly sold 10% more, our gross national product would increase by 1.1 trillion dollars! That is a 10% increase, and a typical "good" increase is only 3%! We can all afford to go back to class now!

W is for Want

Everybody wants something!

When a person decides in their mind that they should own something, they want it. If they buy it or not depend upon two things: the price, and the value.

There are many different words to describe how much people are attracted to something. When we learn about something for the first time, we become <u>aware</u> of it. Then we consider it, and if we are attracted to that item, we <u>like</u> it. When the attraction grows strong enough that we are ready to take action to make it our own, then we <u>want</u> it. Wanting something is the first step in buying it.

When people cannot live without something, they <u>need</u> it. People buy things they need without anyone asking them. They will shop around to find the best prices, but they buy food, gasoline, clothing and shelter whenever they need them. People just cannot do without the necessities. On the other hand, people buy the things they *want* when the time suits them, and only when they believe the value they receive outweighs the price they must pay.

Want is peer reviewed. How does an attraction grow from something a person likes to something a person wants? It usually happens with help from other people. When a person likes something, he or she may bring it up in conversation. The people in the conversation express their opinions on the product. The group discusses the product and sets standards. If the group approves of the product, the person who brought it up becomes more attracted to it. (We take comfort in numbers.) On the other hand, if the group disapproves, the first person becomes less attracted to the product. Sometimes, very rarely, the group that approves of a product grows so large so quickly that a fad occurs. People have bought a lot of silly stuff because of the power of a fad. Do you still have a dusty skateboard somewhere that you cannot ride? I do!

One basic way advertising works is to show other people who want the product too. Commercials and print ads are full of smiling people who want a particular product. The message of those ads is this - Be one of us! We are happy because we have this product! Advertisers hope that someone who sees the ads will emotionally join the group and change from liking the product to wanting the product. Other people want the product, so it must be good.

To sell effectively, focus on what your customer wants. Ask questions to discover what they want. Then you can quickly show them how your product can fulfill that want. Do you see how important questions are to selling effectively? It is a shame that so many salespeople present their products without even asking what the customer wants. That is a waste of time. Since customers will quickly buy the things they want, spend your valuable time 1) asking what they want and 2) explaining how your product does what they want.

In selling, the most important thing about your product is this –

it is not important.

What is important in selling is what the customer wants to buy!

X is for the X-factor: Attitude

Believe you can and you will,
believe you can't and you won't.

[Warning: Attitude is an extremely powerful force. Do not operate attitude if you are taking medication or are under the influence of alcohol. Unexpected success can result from the proper use of attitude.]

People who understand attitude have an unfair advantage over those who do not. After ASK, attitude may be the most important basic concept of selling. That is why there are many books available on the subject. This chapter teaches you how to make attitude work for you.

What exactly is attitude? Attitude is your inner feelings expressed in outer actions. If you feel happy inside, you begin to smile. If you are calm or angry, determined or confused, bold or frightened, etc. your face shows that, too. The expression on your face is normally a good indicator of your attitude. The ways you sit, stand, walk, talk, dress, work or relax change with your attitude, too. Unless you make a conscious decision to disconnect them, your behavior will reflect your attitude.

The fundamental purpose of attitude is to communicate your inner feelings nonverbally. Dogs are nature's best example of attitude. Anybody can immediately tell the difference between "happy, come and play" dog and "angry, stay away" dog. Of course, people are much more sophisticated than dogs. We can mask our inner feelings and we can adjust them. Later in this chapter, you will learn how to do exactly that. In any case, people around you judge if you are "safe" to approach based on your positive or negative attitude.

If your inner feelings and outward actions: 1) make you approachable, 2) help you work with others, and 3) help you successfully accomplish your current responsibilities, people will say you have a positive attitude. If your inner feelings and outward actions keep others away and keep you from success, others will say you have a negative attitude. In sales, your success depends on customers that want to buy from you. A positive attitude makes you approachable and helpful, just the kind of salesperson customers want. A positive salesperson sells more.

Attitude affects all areas of your life, and it operates 24 hours a day. Only one person controls your attitude. You do! You can turn it on, and you can turn it off. You can adjust it whenever you want, if you know how attitude works.

Here is the key to controlling your attitude. Inner feelings affect outward actions directly and strongly. *That connection works both ways!* If you change one, you affect the other. This is a very useful tool. It allows you to control and adjust your attitude from the outside.

The easiest way to change your inner feelings is to change your outer actions. Positive outer actions produce positive inner feelings. If you smile, you begin to feel happy. If you help somebody, you feel better for doing it. If you do something, anything well, you feel better about yourself. Doing good things gives you good inner feelings. Good inner feelings communicate to the outside world as a positive attitude.

What inner feelings can help you sell? Here are a few: trustworthy, loyal, helpful, friendly, courteous, kind, obedient, cheerful, thrifty, brave, clean and reverent. ("Hello," to all the other Scouts who are reading this book. Thanks!) The 12 positive attributes above are The Scout Law, and they are all positive. Of course, you can select any positive attributes to incorporate into your life. It does not matter where they come from. What matters is their quality. Many successful salespeople live by the "Golden Rule – Do unto others as you would have them do unto you." Helping others is a wonderfully positive attribute for salespeople. It keeps them focused on what their customers want. The more positive inner feelings people have, the less room there will be for negative feelings.

Attitude is contagious! Strong attitudes affect weaker ones. Other people are naturally attracted to a happy person, a person with a strong positive attitude. An angry person with a strong negative attitude repels people. Customers are always more likely to buy your product when you have a positive attitude.

When you start any sale, it is natural to feel unsure about yourself. Will the customer say "Yes?" Will they buy? Everyone who has something to sell feels this way. Successful salespeople immediately answer those inner questions with a resounding YES! Unsuccessful salespeople think to themselves, "Maybe they won't." You can think yourself out of a successful sale before you contact your first customer. To prevent that, immediately replace any negative thoughts that enter your head with positive ones.

The "Yes, they will buy from me," salespeople start earlier, make more sales calls and sell more. Those positive salespeople receive a wonderful "I won!" feeling every time their customers say yes. That positive, victorious feeling boosts a positive attitude and gives any salesperson added confidence to sell more.

On the other hand, the "Maybe they won't buy from me," salesperson will procrastinate. They will start later and make fewer calls. When a customer tells them no, it reinforces their negative attitude. Then that negative salesperson believes, "I was right; no one is going to buy." Those negative inner feelings make the salesperson even more unsure and stressed. Other customers recognize that negative attitude and buy less. This process continues until it ends in complete failure. *Avoid this situation!* Start today to adjust your attitude and make it positive!

Always remember that inner feelings express outwardly. Customers easily detect attitudes. Your attitude affects the buyer's response to your selling proposal. This can work for you or against you. A buyer may say yes to a bumbling, positive salesperson. A buyer may say no to a very polished negative salesperson. Routinely, customers will avoid salespeople with bad attitudes and look for salespeople with good attitudes.

Here is a brief example. Occasionally, you must buy things you need (like gasoline or groceries) from a checkout clerk with a bad attitude. They make it obvious that they do not care about you. They do not want to be there and they do not care if you shop there. You just hate to give them your business! If you can avoid shopping there in the future, you probably do.

On the other hand, you enjoy buying the same items from a pleasant happy-to-help sales clerk. With everything else the same, the bad attitude clerk makes you want to shop somewhere else, and the good attitude clerk makes you want to shop there again. Keep this in mind when you are the one selling. Customers respond to your attitude. Keep it positive and sell more!

Y is for Yes

The most beautiful word in the world!

"YES" is the word salespeople work to hear. "Yes" means the customer agrees. "Yes" means that your product is "sold"! (Of course, we know the deal is never really over until you have their money!)

Customers usually tell you they like your product before actually saying, "Yes, I will that buy that today." These little signs of agreement show you that the customer is moving toward buying. Salespeople look for these buying signs along the way to a sale. The more buying signs you see, the closer you are to making the sale.

Statements like these indicate your customer's interest:

"That sounds good."

"Tell me more about that."

"I have always wanted one of those."

Buying signs can also be in the form of questions. Serious questions like these tell you the customer is indeed interested in your product or service.

"How much does that cost?"

"Does it come with any options?"

"Can I get it in yellow?" (Or any other color, size, etc.)

As the salesperson, you can sell more by always responding to a customer's "yes" with some positive statement. You want to make customers feel good about what they just said. Psychologists call this positive reinforcement. Reinforce every buying sign. Make the customers comfortable with the little steps they are taking toward the sale. If a customer says, "That is a great color," you reinforce with something like, "You're right," or "Many of our customers think so." A small reinforcement keeps the sale rolling. If you go overboard with too much, however, the customer will think you are pushing too hard for the sale. This technique works best when it is casual and simple.

When you hear a customer say the first buying sign, prepare to ask them to buy your product. If the first buying sign is a very strong one, like, "I love this!" go ahead and close the deal buy asking them to buy. They may say yes. If they do not say yes right away, then continue to explain another benefit until they say another buying sign. Ask them to buy again. Give all customers the opportunity to say yes after they have given you two buying signs. (Keep in mind that many customers say no. That is fine. When that happens you immediately ask why, and keep the conversation going. You will have a chance to overcome their reason for saying no by adding more benefits.) When they believe the value of your product is worth more than the price, they will say yes and they will buy. This formula works. Either the customer says yes, or they end the conversation before you can show them enough value to make the sale.

Be ready to show customers plenty of benefits. The more a product costs, the more a customer expects you to work for the sale. Does it not make sense that someone spending $1000 should expect more attention than someone spending $10 should?

If you want your buyers to say yes, you must give them *just enough* information to outweigh their no. Give them too little, and they will not buy. Give them too much, and they will not buy. The trick is giving them just enough information. Here is an example.

A customer walks into a store to buy a new television. He asks the first salesperson he sees for some help. "The TVs are over there,' says the first salesman as he walks away to take his morning coffee break. The customer does not buy from him. (Duh!)

The second salesperson is in the TV section. She makes a wonderful first impression by greeting the customer immediately and asking if she can help him buy a TV. "Yes, please," he replies. For the next 35 minutes, he follows her around the TV department, looking at every TV and learning everything there is to know about modern television. The salesperson enjoys teaching people about TVs, and customer is enjoying leaning about it all. Suddenly, he looks at his watch and exclaims, "I have to be at an appointment in two minutes! I am so sorry, I completely lost track of time. All I really wanted was a small color TV to go in my kitchen." The he literally runs out of the store.

The second salesperson may or may not get that sale. She hopes the customer will come back later. If only she had asked questions at first, to discover what the customer wanted! Without that information, she treated a $400 customer as if he was a $4000 customer. She ended up with a $0 customer.

Take your last break! **Sold!**

Even though only a small percentage of people are professional salespeople, nearly everything around us sold at least once. Except for the people, some of the animals around you and the air you breathe, what else do you eat, drink, wear, use, drive or come into contact with that has not sold at least once? Really, think about this for a minute. We pay for our food. We pay for a place to live, water to drink and sewer service. We pay for lights and electricity. We pay for heating and cooling. Someone, at some time, has paid for every acre of land in the United States. That means all the trees, flowers and animals on that land sold at least once.

Selling can be as simple as a can of beans sitting on a grocery store shelf with a price sticker on it. Selling can be as complicated as a multi-year bidding process involving major corporate contractors partnering to win a large government job. Most selling takes place somewhere in between.

It is hard to think of anything that has not sold at least once, and a salesperson is involved in every sale. Selling is definitely the engine that drives business. As a salesperson, you hold your future and the fate of your business in your hands.

OK, this last break is over. It is time to finish the book!

Z is for Zebra

Zebra? Yes. No kidding. Now, please pay attention.

This last point is very important.

Imagine a herd of zebras stampeding across an African valley. Thousands of zebras are all running together, and it looks like a sea of stripes. One zebra, however, at the front of the herd, is completely black. Which zebra immediately captures your attention?

You notice the black zebra, of course. Why? It is different. It has black stripes that are just a little wider than the other zebras. It has stripes that almost touch each other. That is what makes it appear black. It is still a zebra, not an elephant or a giraffe, so it can run with the herd. It is just a little more of a zebra than the rest. The black zebra automatically captures attention wherever it goes.

Now imagine a herd of salespeople all trying to get the attention of one buyer. There may be hundreds of them. All of them are salespeople, not cowboys or astronauts. How can one salesperson stand out from the rest and capture the buyer's attention? By being the black zebra. All zebras have stripes, but the black zebra's stripes are just a little wider. All salespeople use some of these basic concepts of selling, but some salespeople use them just a little better. That is how excellent salespeople gain attention. That is why some salespeople seem to get all the sales. It is not magic and it is not luck. They are just better at the basics!

No matter what type of selling you do, you want to be the black zebra in the herd. You want the attention of the people you are trying to persuade. It does not matter if you are a politician stumping for votes, or a manager, or a coach building a team, or a parent or a teacher, you need other people to believe in the value of your ideas. You need to be more persuasive. You need those people to pay attention to you.

As you learn to apply the alphabetical basic concepts of selling, you will become more persuasive. People will be more likely to accept the value in your ideas. People will follow where you lead them. Buyers will appreciate you more than they do other salespeople. They will buy from you instead of others, because you care more about what they want to buy instead of what you need to sell. Your managers will pay attention to you, too, as they notice your growing sales. Eventually, everyone will pay more attention to you as you become the black zebra!

Practice using one of the basic concepts every day. You will get better with them as you use them and see positive results. In twenty-six days, you will find yourself applying more and more of the basics in your selling. It does not happen overnight, and that is okay. It will happen over time. The more you practice, the sooner you will see results. The more you practice, the wider your stripes will become. Keep it up, and enjoy selling more!

A word of caution to all you black zebras out there. Lions notice you, too, so you better keep running! When you are the black zebra, or the top salesperson, you are the one everyone wants to beat. That is a great problem to have. It takes extra effort to stay the best, to stay out in front, but it is worth it. The view from the front of the herd is always better than the view from the back. In the back of the herd, you eat dust and stare at the same old zebra rumps all day! Do you want to live like that?

I hope *you* start using these basic concepts of selling, and quickly move toward the front of the herd!

In closing

With knowledge comes great potential,

with <u>action</u> comes great achievement.

Now you know. You know the basic concepts of selling. You know how to sell anything. You know how to be more persuasive. You know how to convince others in the value of your ideas. So what?

The *fact* is that you now know, after reading this simple book, more about selling that most people on this planet do. The *benefit* of that fact is this – *if* you begin using these basic concepts, you can be more persuasive. You can sell more, you can earn more and your customers will have greater respect for you. The key word here is *if*. Now it depends on you to take action. Go. Call. Visit. Write. *You* must contact a customer before any of these basic concepts can work for you.

Will you please start using these basic concepts of selling today?

I have a strong feeling that you will. Good luck to you, and good selling!

About the author

Growing up in Minden, Louisiana, Dale was an Eagle Scout, lifeguard and an internationally competitive target shooter. He earned a *summa cum laude* degree in Educational Psychology in 1978. Entering the U.S. Army, Dale advanced to the rank of Captain, becoming a nuclear and chemical weapons expert. Dale became a pharmaceutical salesman in 1983, and sold prescription drugs for pharmaceutical giants Johnson & Johnson and Glaxo. He joined a small drug company, Russ Pharmaceuticals, in Birmingham, AL in 1987. He managed marketing for LORTAB® pain reliever as it went national and became one of America's top-100 prescribed drugs. Later, as a Russ sales manager in Cleveland, Ohio, Dale hired and trained new salespeople for the mid-west.

In 1990, Dale and seven others founded their own pharmaceutical company, Scandipharm, to treat cystic fibrosis. In the first year, Dale sold over a million dollars of new products while simultaneously performing the company's national marketing duties. For the next 8 years, as the Director of Marketing, then Director of National Account Sales and Director of Managed Healthcare Sales, Dale helped grow annual sales to $65 million dollars. After Scandipharm sold in 2000, Dale became the Vice-President of Business Development for Channel Link, a national e-commerce pharmaceutical software development firm. When that company sold, Dale enjoyed a year off, and then went to work for The Birmingham News Company. As the newspaper Sales Manager for Retail Advertising, Dale hires, trains and manages advertising salespeople who work with all businesses to provide effective newspaper, direct mail and internet advertising. Dale is a regular contributor to national advertising web forums, and he is currently President-Elect of the Birmingham Chapter of the American Advertising Federation.

Dale has over 30 years of success in sales, marketing, management and training. Throughout that time, he used his training in psychology to observe and record the common behaviors of award-winning salespeople. The results of his observations are the basis for this book.

If you would like to contact Dale, please send your email to:
dale@alphabeticalbasicconcepts.com